Opportunistic Millionaire 2.0

It doesn't matter where you are; it only matters where you're going

Shawn Ousley

Dedication / Introduction

This book is dedicated to you. Yes you. This book is dedicated to you the person who is about to make the rest of their life the best of their life.

The first edition of Opportunistic Millionaire was dedicated to the late Dr. Jerry Blackman, who over the course of eleven years conversed, advised, and taught me many things. Two things that he said will forever stay with me. The first statement was: No matter what you do, you must have a plan. The second words of wisdom I shall always remember are: There are 500 ways a day to make money; it's up to you to find them.

Over the past few years I have taken these two statements, put them together and realized how so many people miss out on opportunities in life. I have come to understand that anyone can be a millionaire as long as they have a plan. Along with having a plan, a person must also focus on opportunities, as well as develop their skills. In addition to those steps, it is essential they learn to properly manage their time and money.

This is not a get-rich-quick book. I do not wish to promote to you a get-rich-quick concept. However, this book is a step in the right direction to get you where you want to be in life. Living check to check, robbing Peter to pay Paul, barely keeping your head above water, are all clichés when someone is struggling to keep the bills paid and food on the table. My wish is for everyone who reads this book to get an idea in his or her head. And with that idea, state that they are and will be an Opportunistic Millionaire.

In life I have seen people with great skills make money for other people or they use their skills as a side gig to make a few extra dollars. Every person has a skill, a trade, or an ability that would make it possible for them to be their own boss, write their own ticket, and sign their own paycheck. But why do they not do so? Are they scared? Or do they not have a plan?

This book is for you. Yes there is more than one copy, but this copy is for you. Why? Because throughout this book you will write words, phrases, and answers that pertain to you alone. This book will be your guide to get started on your path you set for yourself.

Follow Your Passion / Follow Your Dream

Table of Content

Chapter 1 – What is an Opportunistic Millionaire?

First let's get the formal definition of the two words that make up the title. Afterwards we will talk about the joint definition. Then we will discuss what this means to you. Opportunistic by definition means taking advantage of opportunities: taking advantage of an opportunity, or exploiting opportunities and situations in general. Another definition of opportunistic is taking immediate advantage of any circumstance of possible benefit. Now that we have the definition of opportunistic I would like to say that in no way am I condoning any unethical or illegal activities. Millionaire by definition is somebody who has a net worth or income that is more than one million dollars, pounds, or another unit of currency.

Now pause for a moment and put those two definitions together in your own words. Write down your collective definition of Opportunistic Millionaire.

_____

_____

_____

_____

For this book the following definition will be used: An opportunistic millionaire is a person who understands what it takes to get to where they want to be financially, and puts themselves in places to make their financial goals happen as well as keep their eyes and ears open for any opportunity that comes their way. It is my belief that everyone has the capability to be an opportunistic millionaire. I believe that anyone who wants to be financially stable should be financially stable. Moreover, anyone who wants to be financially stable can achieve financial stability. The question now is: What steps should be taken to become and opportunistic millionaire?

This concept first started when my wife and I moved to Charlotte, North Carolina after I accepted a state government job. We were in a two-bedroom apartment with our two sons. My wife was a stay-at-home mom and wanted to do something to make a few extra dollars. We thought of so many things that we/she could do to generate some extra income from home. After a few weeks of brain storming it finally hit me one night while I was in a hotel room: Why not do all of them. And that is exactly what we decided to do.

Nothing was stopping us from trying all of our ideas. You may ask what our ideas were. Well...1) Buying or getting for free old wood furniture and refinishing it and then selling it. 2) Separating and selling my extensive sports' card collection. 3) Buying old comic books at low prices and then reselling them to collectors. 4) Buying gently used clothes from yard sales, online, etc... then selling them to consignment shops or online. 5) Looking out for items people set on the road to fix and resell. 6) Helping writers get their works published. 7) Finding deals at thrift stores and yard sales and then selling the items to collectors. Did all of these ideas work? Yes. Did each one make us a millionaire? No. However, doing these things started us in the right direction. Doing these income making strategies were fun, and it gave us more than those few extra dollars she wanted to make.

Extra Income Checklist

1 – Refurbish wood furniture
2 – Sell sport's cards
3 – Comic book flipping
4 – Sell clothes
5 – Road pickup
6 – Publish others
7 – Item flipping

As you see in the picture on the previous page, the first concept of opportunistic millionaire was doing as many things as possible to make as much money as possible. We soon realized that we had to focus on what worked best. Along with that, we didn't know where the extra money was going to go to. Why were we creating extra income without knowing what the money was going toward? What was our plan for the money? What were our goals or were we just doing it for fun?

For us, we had to make a plan. That plan was to save enough money to buy three four-unit apartment buildings (four-plex) and retire before 2024. Why 2024? In 2024 I will turn 45, and both of our sons would be out of the house. Once we have ownership of three four-plexes, nothing can stop us from buying more four-plexes each time we save up enough money to purchase another one. As long as we keep our eyes focused on our goals nothing can stop us from achieving the goals we have destined for ourselves. Our long-term plan is to transfer ownership of a four-plex to each of our sons. We have the understanding that it would be better to leave our sons a four-plex than money. Why? If you leave a child money they may spend it or maybe they will save it. However, if we leave each of our sons a four-plex, then they will have residual income coming to them every month. The options are we leave them $150,000 each or a four-plex worth $150,000. Well if they put the money in a savings account then there is no way they can live off of the interest. However, with the four-plex they can comfortably receive an income of $2600-$4000 a month. My wife and I are striving to reach that goal as well as implant that mindset into our sons.

That is our plan, which may not work for everyone. But what will work for everyone is determination. Determination to get to where they want to be will work for everyone. Out of all of the millionaires in the United States, over 80% of them are self-made millionaires. That means that anyone, yes anyone, can be a millionaire. The difference between a millionaire and a non-millionaire is in how they work and think.

Taking responsibility is an essential part of changing how you think. Understanding that you have complete control over your life and you and only you are responsible for what happens in your life. The self-made millionaires in the United States decided to take responsibility over their lives and strive for greatness. You literally have to start thinking differently to be an opportunistic millionaire. You have to start looking more at needs and not wants. Too many people live at the mall on the weekend buying all of the things they want and not saving for what they need. Too many people focus on right now and never have a long-term plan. To be an opportunistic millionaire one must have a plan and think long term.

To be an opportunistic millionaire a person has to break bad habits and start new habits. Eating out numerous times a week, buying items from the vending machine, buying a cup of coffee each day could be considered by some as bad financial habits. On the other hand being frugal, penny pinching, and couponing could be considered good habits by some. It's easy to point out the bad habits of others. However, I challenge you to look at your own bad habits. Now, I challenge you to look at your bad financial habits. Once a person can point out their own bad financial habits, they are on the right track to start changing those habits. When a person has acquired better financial habits they are on their way to becoming financially secure and on the right track to becoming an opportunistic millionaire.

End of chapter thoughts
Write down what each statement means to you.

The time has not passed to be what you could have been.

Obstacles are those things that you see when you take your focus off of your goal.

When you are stuck between a rock and a hard place, keep moving forward.

Chapter 2 – Goals

Once again let's start with the definition. The formal definition of the word goal is something that somebody wants to achieve. Another definition of the word goal states the purpose toward which an endeavor is directed.

I remember seeing a man going through the garbage at a gas station one day looking for cans. I asked him what he were his plans with the money once he cashed in the cans. He stated to me that this was how he bought his cigarettes. He said that he decided to stop spending his own money to buy cigarettes. I asked him how much cans were going for. He answered about two cents per can. I thought that was an intriguing idea so I asked the man how was his plan working for him. He said that he was smoking less and saving money. He added that people throw away so much and that on any given day he may find a few dollars balled up in a discarded receipt. However, he stated that the cash he finds goes to other things. He only buys cigarettes with the money he gets from cashing in cans. Doing the math, if he smoked 3 packs a week at $5 a pack, that would be $15 a week or $780 a year. So with his plan he is saving $780 a year of his own money and getting a bonus of the balled up cash in receipts.

You may be asking what this story has to do with goals. Well this is a simple plan or endeavor, which has a definite and achievable goal. This man had a plan. He created a strategy to carry out the plan, and has clear cut goals. How does this apply to being an opportunistic millionaire? On a slightly larger scale, you will have to develop a plan, create a strategy, and have clear cut defined goals. Just working until something happens will not get you anywhere. However having a goal to work toward gives you something to focus on each day.

Jane wants to open her own used book store. That statement alone tells us Jane's goal – to own a used book store. She has saved

$22,000 over the past four years just for this goal. The next step is what strategy Jane will use to achieve this goal. Jane decides that she wants to open in six months, and would like to have a few seats for customers where they can sit and meet. Jane chooses to shop at local thrift stores and browse craigslist and the classifieds for local yard sales to get her initial inventory. Her plan is to make sure she has everything she needs before she even starts moving into her business facility. Jane has a plan to get her inventory, and a plan to store the inventory, as well as a plan on how she wants to setup the inside of her store.

With only the information you know about Jane, what other goals do you think she should have for herself?
1)_____
2)_____
3)_____
4)_____

What does setting goals do for you? Setting goals keep your mind sharp. When your mind is not working, then it may stop working. Not literally, but if you do not use your "thinking cap" then it may fly off. Setting goals improves a person's self-confidence. Individuals who set goals and then achieve the goals feel better about themselves. It does not matter what scale you set your goals on; the important thing is that you have a goal and work towards the goal. Once the goal is set the hard part comes next – achieving the goal. This step is what makes an opportunistic millionaire different from the person who just has a goal.

This next step, achieving the goal, has so many barriers that many give up and go back to their old routine of dreaming and not pursuing. When the time comes for you to start working toward achieving the goal that you have set for yourself many obstacles will arise. I would like to tell you right now the difference between those who achieve their goals and those who don't. Those who achieve their goals always move forward and let nothing stop them from achieving their goal. Those that don't achieve their goals find reasons to let excuses stop them from moving forward.

Let's take a look back at Jane. What obstacles could possibly get in the way of Jane achieving her goal of starting a used book store? First, there could be a shortage of books for sale at the local yard sales. The books at the thrift stores could be over priced or in bad condition. There may not be available commercial rental space in her price range. These three obstacles would and will hinder many from starting a used book store. However, Jane found a way around these obstacles. First, Jane went to each thrift store and filled a cart up with all of the books she wanted. She then asked to speak to the manager. Once she was with the manager, she offered a fair price for the entire lot of books that she had in the cart. When it came to yard sales, Jane decided to use the yard sales not only for books but also for furniture she could reupholster for the customer seating. Jane decided that she should try other ways to locate a commercial rental for her used book store.

Jane started calling all of the vacant spaces for rent and asking them if they would take what she had to offer. She understood that the worst answer she could get was "No". She was able to find an owner who loved books and gave her a discount only if Jane agreed to let him hold networking meetings there once a month. She agreed and the networking meetings have helped bring in more business to her used book store.

What financial and non-financial goals do you have in your life?
1)_____
2)_____
3)_____
4)_____

Why do you want to be a millionaire?
_____

What are you going to do once you achieve your goals?

_____

What strategies do you have to reach your goals?

_____

There are those who say that goal setting doesn't work. I agree with them to a certain degree. Goal setting doesn't work when a person sets a goal that has no definitive purpose. Goal setting does not work when the person gives up when obstacles arise. Goal setting doesn't work when you do not write down your goals. These three things are the reasons I see that goal setting does not work. However, if a person writes out a definite pin-pointed goal and works around every obstacle, they will achieve their goal.

End of chapter thoughts
Write down what each statement means to you.

Knowing where you want to be is the first step to getting where you want to be.

Let go of whatever is stopping you from reaching your dream.

Chapter 3 – Keeping Your Eyes and Ears Open

This could well be the most important chapter in this book. Why you ask? The most important factor of being an opportunistic millionaire is knowing when an opportunity is presenting itself to you. Remember the statement, "There are 500 ways a day to make money; it's up to you to find them". In other words your eyes and ears should be open at all times and without hesitation you should know whenever and opportunity is presenting itself to you.

Mitch wanted to add some extra money to his retirement account. He thought about getting a second job, but didn't want to punch a clock. He liked the idea of starting a side business, but he wanted to work the business from home. Mitch sat down and thought about what he could do with what he already had. After a while, he decided to start a weekend truck-for-hire service. Mitch thought about all of the people who had called him over the past few years to ask him to move items for them. Mitch then planned out his strategy.
1) Get business cards made
2) Visit stores that sell large items but do not deliver
3) Post his services on Facebook and Craigslist
4) Visit fire wood sellers

Mitch had a simple plan with a definite goal. He knew what he wanted to do and who his potential customer base was. However, Mitch kept his eyes and ears open everywhere he went. While at dinner with his wife and daughter, Mitch overheard a man talking to his wife about how they were given five free shrubs but had no way to pick them up. Mitch turned to the couple and stated that he overheard their dilemma and handed them one of his business cards. That weekend Mitch added $100 to his retirement account courtesy of the couple. On the weekends that Mitch has nothing booked, he drives through parking lots and look for individuals struggling to place large items in their cars. He says that he usually get a few customers a weekend while parking lot cruising.

No matter where you are, you should always keep a lookout for an opportunity. I remember when my wife and I decided to sell items on craigslist for extra income. Every time we left our house, we kept our eyes wide open to see what people had thrown out. The times that we picked the items up, we would fix the items then sell the item. Other times we would simply clean the item and sell it. At no point did we spend our own money to get these items. Many, if not all of the items, we would pick up on our way to and from school, work, or the store. I remember two yard sales that we had where many of the items were road side discards that people did not want. Not only did we make extra money doing this, but we also enjoyed doing this. As time went on, we learned more and more about various items, their worth, and how easy the items are to sell.

You don't have to know everything about everything. No one knows everything about every single thing. However, it's good to know 1 or 2 things about many things. Many would be surprised how much they really knew if they had to write it down. Just think real fast about two things you know about the following items:
1) Decorations
2) Home and office furniture
3) Movies
4) Audio devices - vinyl records, cassettes, CD's
5) Clothing
6) Musical instruments
7) Cook ware
8) Toys - new and old
9) Comic books
10) Tools

Now go back over the list and try to think of 10 things you know about each of the items listed above. If you can think of 10 things you know about the 10 items listed above, that's 100 facts you have in your head, right now. The items listed above are the basic items needed to start a thrift store. Knowing 1 or 2 facts about various things comes in handy in all forms of business. For those who deal in second-hand sales this is very important. For those who decide to buy storage lockers (something many people buy), this knowledge is pivotal in whether they should bid on a storage locker or not. Others who own thrift stores keep their eyes and ears open for upcoming estate sells and yard sales.

When people decide to always keep their eyes and ears open, they do the following:
- Know what others have stated a need for
- Know what others are selling
- Know what people are willing to buy
- Know what others are giving away
- Know what has "at price" value to one person, and "collector's" value to another
- Know their clientele

There is never a bad time to start doing better. Use the skills that you currently possess and get started being whatever you want to be. Use your current skills to start living how you want to live. Use your current skills to start the path toward buying that house or condo where you want to stay. What skills do you currently possess? Think long and hard about all of the skills that you have. What hobbies do you have that others may see as a skill? Could any of your current skills generate income?

Many people spend their time doing home repairs. Others enjoy doing wood work in their garage or workshop. How easy would it be to turn those skills into a business? A person who loves woodworking could start a business repairing fences or decks. If the same person had interest in broadening their clientele they could transform that business into a handyman business. On the next page is a list of skills and hobbies that can be used to start a business. In the column to the right put a mark next to the skill/hobby that you have.

Skill /Hobby	X
Automotive repairs	
Baking	
Camping	
Chess	
Coin Collecting	
Couponing	
Crafts	
Drawing	
Fishing (yes, fishing)	
Fitness	
Gardening	
Hiking	
Organizing	
Planning	
Playing an instrument	
Photography	
Quilting	
Reading	
Sewing	
Shopping (yes, shopping)	
Woodworking	
Writing	

It should be stated that every hobby/skill was not listed. However, look at what you have checked. What group of people could you market your hobby/skill to? If you kept your eyes and ears open, who else could you market your skill/hobby to? If you are freelancing there is nothing wrong with having more than one hobby/skill that generates income. As stated before my wife and I were doing more than five extra-income endeavors at the same time and all of them were working. You must stay focused and keep your eyes and ears open.

There are so many shows on television showing the many ways people are generating income from businesses they have started. There are individuals who hunt alligators for 30 days a year. In those 30 days they generate over 80% of their yearly income. Another show has people who search for junk and then resale the items they find for a profit. There are at least 3 shows about families that have started and run their own pawn shops. On more than one network there are shows that depict investors who buy old homes, fix and remodel the homes, and then sell the homes for profit. At last count there are at least four shows where people buy abandoned storage units and sell the content for profit. Whenever a person watches any of these shows they should think would they be able to do the same. Do they have the skill to generate income by mimicking what they are seeing on television? Or better yet, do they have skills that are better and can generate more income than what they are seeing on television? The shows are on television for entertainment, however much can be learned from the shows. While watching shows that depict how others make a living, one should try to learn something. Try to pick up on some of what they are doing. If the show has more than one entrepreneur point out to yourself the good and bad qualities in each entrepreneur. There is something that can be learned from watching others create income.

End of chapter thoughts

Write down three skills/hobbies that you have and how using that skill/hobby can generate income for you.

1)_____

_____

_____

_____

_____

2)_____

_____

_____

_____

_____

3)_____

_____

_____

_____

_____

Chapter 4 – Self Development: Read, Learn, and Ask

By definition self-development is the development of one's capabilities or potentialities, or the state or process of improving or developing oneself. There are three ways a person can develop themselves: read, learn, and ask.

Let's start with reading. What should you read? Everything. Yes, everything. This may seem a bit extreme, but reading everything would increase your overall general knowledge. Reading everything will also introduce you to activities and ideas that you may have never known fascinated you.

Since I was 14 years old my mom has bought me an Almanac for Christmas along with other gifts. At first I thought this was weird and a crazy gift. Fast forward a few days after that first Christmas that I received that massive book as a gift. I picked it up to just flip through the pages to see what the book was all about. I was surprised to say the least. Anyone who has ever opened up an almanac knows the vast knowledge that it contains. The almanac is what got me started with wanting to know "Jeopardy"-type information. I learned many things from reading the almanac. The most interesting thing that stands out from when I first opened the almanac is about the small European country Luxemburg. What's interesting is that I read about this country in Europe, and then when studying Europe in school, the teacher divided up all of the countries among the class for each student to do a one-page report. To my surprise I got Luxemburg.

Reading everything consists of magazines you wouldn't normally read, articles about events that have no meaning to you, night time stories to the kids in your family, books from a genre that you wouldn't normally read, everything. Again, reading everything introduces you to things you may actually like but didn't know you liked.

Read books about money. If you want to make money and live a better-than-comfortable life, read about money. I am fascinated by how people make money. Anytime I see an article about how a person made millions before a certain age, I read it. Books about money are very interesting. There are many points that stand out when people talk about the differences between millionaires and non-millionaires. Reading is the one item on the list that always stands out to me. One columnist stated that rich people read for education and learning, while poor people read for entertainment. What do you read, and why do you read it? Many people believe that what goes on in Washington DC does not concern them personally. They are far from wrong. Every time congress and the senate decide to add a tax, up a rate, increase, or decrease something, you should read about it.

Once you have pinpointed the area in which your goal is set start reading in your field. Make a goal to read a minimum of thirty minutes a day. Reading in your field every day will put you ahead of your competition no matter your field. Reading in your field will keep you up to date on the happenings in your field. Extra benefits of reading include reduced stress, expanded vocabulary, and helps improve your memory.

Would you start a business without researching the business? In today's world you can research anything you want by typing the subject in a search engine online. If a person is focusing on one certain item to buy or sale, it would be wise for that person to read about everything they can about that subject. Every written resource available about a subject should be used by a person to achieve their goals.

Kent, after long nights of thinking and weighing the pros and cons of different businesses to open decided to start a lawn care business. Kent sat down in front of his computer to read everything he could find concerning the lawn care business. Kent typed the following in his search engine of choice:

- How to start a lawn care business
- How to get new lawn care customers
- How to promote a lawn care business
- How to advertise a lawn care business
- Getting commercial lawn care accounts
- How to cut lawns properly
- How high should grass be after cutting
- How to properly seed a lawn
- Equipment needed to start a lawn care business
- What are the best push mowers
- What are the best riding mowers
- What are the best zero-turn mowers
- How to bill lawn care customers

Anytime Kent thought of an aspect of lawn care that he hadn't already read about he would look it up. When looking up the different aspects he would read more than one result of his questioning. Reading about all the aspects of lawn care was Kent's way to learn.

Which leads to the next aspect of self-development, learning. While reading about a particular subject a person should be learning something. Besides reading, there are many ways to learn. One way is to take a free class at a local college. Many colleges across the county offer free classes in traditional and non-traditional subjects. Often times the classes are one or two days total, and are taught by someone sharing insight about their hobby or a subject in which they have vast knowledge. Sometimes these classes have a small fee, usually less than $50. Think how it would benefit you to take a one-day class on new advertising methods on the internet if you are trying to get more customers under the age of 30. The $50 investment to take the class would certainly be worth it in the long run. If the classroom isn't for you, taking a free online course may be more your speed. Go to the search engine of your choice and type in "free online class" and see what comes up. I did this simple task and brought up the following free classes:

- Fundamentals of Physics
- Prices
- Modern Poetry
- Producing Films for Social Change
- History of Public Health
- Cattle Management
- African American History
- Capital Markets
- Introduction to Economics
- Microeconomics for Managers
- Spa Operations
- Family Finance
- Fundamentals of Business Analysis

That's just 13 of the over 200 free online classes found just by typing in "free online class" in a search engine. There should be nothing keeping you from learning what you want to learn.

Ken read so much about lawn care, that after about a week of reading, he decided he wanted to watch and listen. He then went to YouTube and typed in "lawn care business". To his surprise there were over 10,000 videos on lawn care on YouTube. So, for those who want to learn from hearing and seeing, watching videos may be their path to self-development. If there were three classes you could take for free, what would they be?

1) _____
2) _____
3) _____

The question now is what is stopping you from taking the class? Go to your search engine of choice and type in "free online class in _____" along with the name of the class you would like to take. Find out what classes the local colleges offer for free or for a small fee.

The final component of self-development is to ask. Many things can happen when people ask a question that will help their self-development. First, the question could be answered in a manner that is helpful to the one asking the question. Second, the question could be answered not-so-right. And lastly, the person being asked does not know the answer. It should be understood that there are no stupid questions. The worst thing that can happen is that the question is not asked at all. In a classroom setting the asking of a question may lead to a greater discussion that will further enlighten the students or class participants. Also, what if a question is asked and others also needed the answer to the same question but they were afraid to ask. Furthermore, in a classroom setting, many questions are more for the need of clarification rather than just a question.

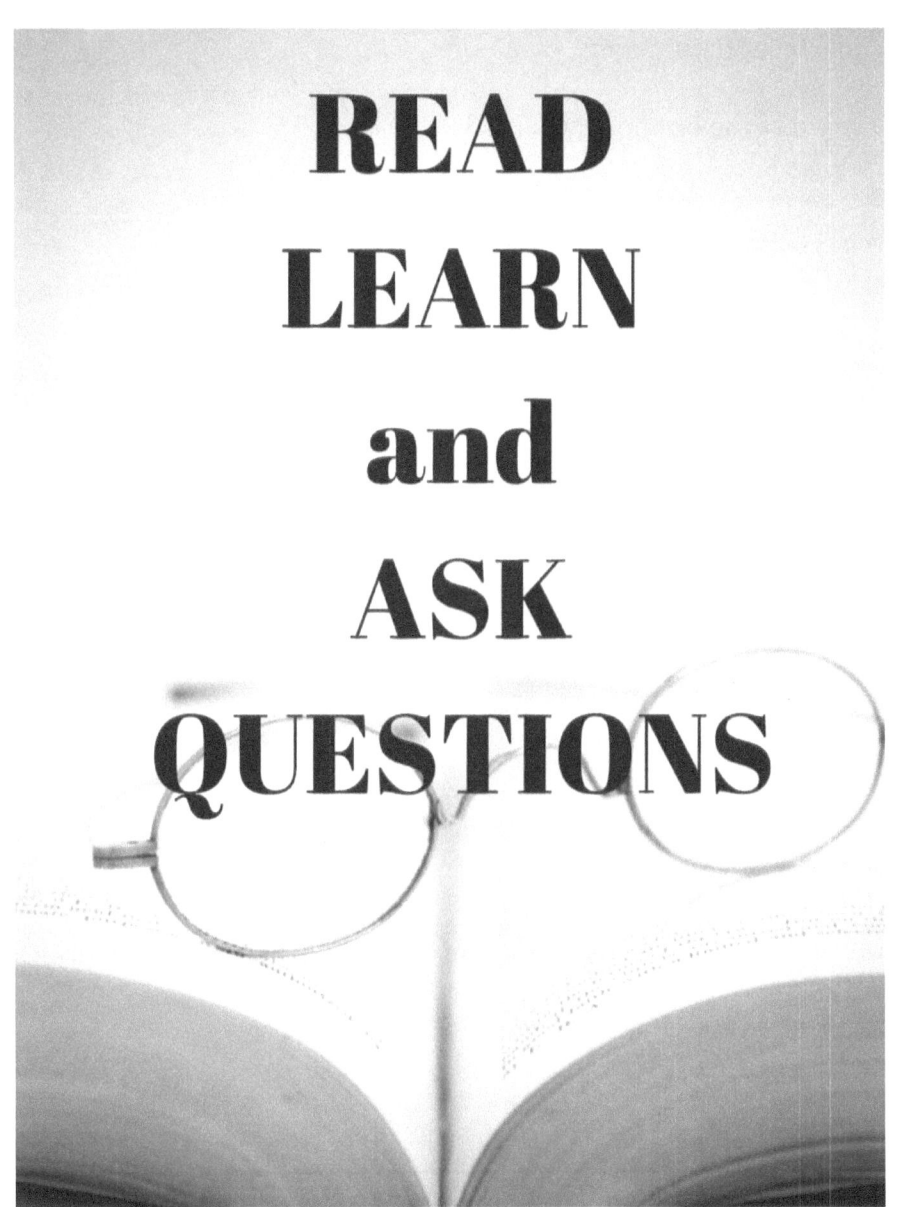

READ

LEARN

and

ASK

QUESTIONS

End of chapter thoughts

What was the last book you read?

What was the reason you read that book?

What was the last thing you read that was educational?

What were you learning about?

What magazines do you read on a regular basis?

What are you learning from these magazines?

What are you really learning from these magazines?

Do you believe that non-entertainment reading can be enjoyable? Why or why not?

Chapter 5 – Time Management

What if someone gave you $1440 a day? You can do whatever you wanted to do with the $1440. Any leftover cash cannot carry over to the next day. Why are we talking about money in a chapter entitled Time Management? Well, from 12 midnight to 12 midnight everyday each person gets 1440 minutes. How those minutes are managed are up to the individual.

Time is the one commodity that everyone has an equal daily amount of. How that time is used separates the opportunistic millionaire from others. How time is managed also separates productive people from nonproductive people. Many office managers choose to have their employees write out what they are doing each minute of the day to show where the employee can make better use of their time at work. Remember Kent, the lawn care business owner. Kent stated that his time management skills have greatly increased since starting his business. When asked why that is, he stated that knowing what needs to be done and prioritizing the work save not only time but money as well. In Kent's case, planning out his daily route before leaving helped him save on driving time and fuel cost.

It is true that a person's bad time management can cause bad money management. Let's say Bob stays up late and watches reruns all night and then wakes up late. Bob then rushes to get cleaned up and out the door to work. While at work he reads about sports and the latest entertainment gossip. Soon the boss is at his door reminding Bob of a report that is due tomorrow morning. After the boss leaves, Bob then looks up menus online to see where he wants to go for lunch. Stop right here for a moment. Write down the time management problems that you see that Bob has.

_____

_____

_____

First, Bob is staying up late watching reruns, which is causing him to wake up late. Since he is rushing out of the house, he is spending money to buy breakfast instead of eating breakfast at home. Instead of getting to work and working, Bob is reading about sports and entertainment gossip. This is the time he should be working on the report that is due the next day. Bob then is worried about lunch. The issue of lunch should have been solved before getting to work. However, Bob could have brought his lunch (more on that in the next chapter) and saved that money as well. Bob's bad time management has caused him to spend money on breakfast and lunch, has gotten him behind on his work, and possibly getting written up at work if the report is not done in a timely fashion.

To reach your financial goal, ask yourself this question: What can I be doing right now to generate income? If you are doing something for more than 30 minutes, ask yourself what did you get out of those 30 minutes. What does one get out of watching music videos for 30 minutes? What does one get from jogging for 30 minutes? What does one get from fishing for 30 minutes? What does one get from showering for 30 minutes? What does one get from reading a money magazine for 30 minutes? What does one get from listening to gossip for 30 minutes? You see where this is going... Everything has an outcome. However, every outcome is not beneficial to an individual who is focused on achieving goals. The same time that a person uses watching television or playing video games could be used in self-development. The same time that a person is wasting 30 minutes could be used to promote their business.

Many people who have bad time management have a variety of time wasters. Time wasters are those things that take up chunks of time that could be used in a productive fashion. Playing two hours of video games is a time waster for many people. The two hours that are being wasted playing video games could be used to market and promote a business. Talking on the phone is a time waster for others. The time used to talk on the phone about unnecessary things can be used to generate income or for self-development.

However, if one must talk on the phone that time can be used to speak about business or to generate leads. Remember everything has an outcome. What is the outcome for someone who goes to a networking meeting? Going to the networking meeting introduces them to other professionals as well as prospective customers.

It is very vital to understand significance of time management. The amount of time in a day will always be 24 hours (or 1440 minutes). Regardless of how things are organized the amount of time in a day will never change. Again despite different opportunities everyone has an equal amount of time, so the only thing that can be done is shift the way time is used. There are many ways to start gaining skills to better manage one's time.

Listed below are ways to have better time management. Mark the time management ideas that you think would work for you.

- Create a daily "To Do List" with a stated time for each task
- Use a daily calendar/daily organizer
- Learn to say "No". Thus, having less to do
- Don't rush, but strive to be on time
- Focus on one task at a time, without multitasking
- Write down how much time you spend doing various tasks
- Prioritize tasks
- Know what your time wasters are
- Do important stuff first
- Identify deadlines for tasks
- Motivate yourself
- Get your clothes ready each night for the next day

Write down three time wasters that you do that are not beneficial for your goals in life.

1) _____
2) _____
3) _____

What can you do to manage your time better and remove these three time wasting activities out of your life?

_____

_____

_____

To summarize, it is extremely important that you apply your time sensibly when focusing on achieving your goal. Planning your day out the night before can help you accomplish more. Doing this will also give you control of what you want to do with your life. When planning out the tasks for the upcoming day prioritize by putting the most important task at the top. Even if you cannot do that task until later into the day, at least you will see the task first when you glance over the list. Keeping a schedule will also help you from having time conflicts. Before you agree to do something, look over your to-do list and think about your goals and schedule them prior to agreeing to taking on a new task. Do not stress over large jobs. Try making a large job into 3 to 10 smaller jobs.

For instance instead of building a fire pit in one big job, one could break the large job down into 3 smaller tasks. Remember that doing a task correctly the first time takes less time than going back and fixing mistakes. Minimize distractions in your life. TV, radio, family, neighbors, and the phone can all be distractions. If there is someone who only calls you to gossip, stop taking the call. Just think about what else you could be doing instead of listening to gossip for 25 minutes. In some cases you may have to close your door and turn your phone off. Yes, off.

Limit your time on the internet. There are many times people get on the internet for one thing that should take only 10 minutes and they end up wasting 2 hours doing nothing productive. Lastly, enjoy life. Yes, you have a goal to achieve, but you also have a life to live and enjoy. Take a few minutes each day and just enjoy what you have and what is around you.

End of chapter thoughts
Write down if you agree with each statement. Explain your answer.

Time is money.

There is only so much that can be done in a day.

Being disorganized causes bad time management.

Chapter 6 – Money Management

There is no way to write a book about money without addressing the issue of money management. The formal definition of money management is the process of budgeting, saving, investing, spending or otherwise in overseeing the cash usage of an individual or group. A simpler definition of money management could be the way a person or group spends and saves their money. Without going into a regurgitated lecture of what others have said about money management let's take another path.

Brea like many people, gripe about the lack of money they have as payday gets closer. The moment Brea gets her paycheck, she is happy and at the store, going out to eat, going to the movies, and enjoying the money she has earned. Brea has yet to realize that her payday spending sprees are causing her to have a lack of funds as the days come closer to her next payday. Yet, Brea goes through this same cycle over and over. As Brea goes through her check to check cycle, her co-worker, Linda is experiencing the same dilemma; however Linda has a budget leak. What is a budget leak? A budget leak is money that is slowly being paid out that is not much but over time adds up to a large amount. How can Linda have a budget leak and her bills are paid on time, yet she too complains about the lack of cash as payday gets closer? Linda's budget leak comes from her morning coffee at $3.50 each, and going out to lunch to eat at $7 a day. Together that's $10.50 a day Linda is spending. Over the course of a week she spends $17.50 on coffee and $35.00 on lunch. Linda is spending $70 a month on coffee and $140 a month on lunch. What could Linda do at the end of the month with an extra $210 in her pocket or bank account?

Linda is an extreme case of a budget leak. Most individuals who have a budget leak do not realize it at all, that's where the word "leak" comes in. If a person goes to the vending machine at work each day and spends 75¢ on snacks is a total of $15 a month (assuming they are off two days a week). Many budgets leaks are caused by cigarettes, soda, candy, lottery tickets, pay-per-view, video rentals, fast food, etc... Budget leaks must be stopped to achieve financial goals. Also, to achieve a financial goal a budget with good money management must be used. Knowing what is important is a step in the right direction when it comes to budgeting and managing ones money.

For the next exercise you will need a calculator or a pencil & paper.

Take a look at the following bills. If you only have $325 left after paying rent/mortgage, in what order would you pay the following bills? Note that $325 is not enough to pay all of the remaining bills.

__Lunch $10

__Gas for Car $40

__Utility Bill $175

__Car Insurance $65

__Cell Phone Bill $65

__Groceries $90

What bill did you mark #1 and why?

What item, if any, did you mark #5 and why?

What bill was not paid and why?

Do you think you and your mate would have different answers for the above 3 questions?

What would be a reason someone would not pay their utility bill from this exercise?

From this exercise, would it be wise to pay the four least expensive bills first? Why or why not?

Here are a few tips for good money management.

1) Pay your bills on time and avoid late fees. Just think how much fun it is to pay out an extra $25 to $100 a month because the bills are late. That's up to $1200 a year in late fees.

2) Pay more than the minimum on your credit cards. As long as you pay the minimum there will always be a principle balance.

3) Speaking of credit cards, pay them off and stop using them.

4) Find the cheapest rate on your insurance policies. If you could save $10 a month on your car insurance, $15 on your homeowners/renter's insurance, and $5 a month on your life insurance, that's $30 a month (or $360 a year).

5) For one month write down every dollar spent (down to the cent). Review the list at the end of the week and see if there are any budget leaks.

6) Write out and follow a monthly budget. The best way to get to where you want to be financially is to write down where you will be spending your money.

7) Check credit card statements and make sure it is correct. You want to make sure that you are only being charged for what you have actually purchased.

8) Read over your bank statements to make sure they line up with what you have. You need to make sure that no other transactions have occurred on your account that you are unaware of. This is a great way to prevent identity theft before it gets too far.

9) Create an emergency fund. Start with a $100 emergency fund. Next, build the fund to $500. Then build to your desired amount.

10) Do not finance. Instead of financing a new living room set for $3000, save whatever amount the payments would be until you have saved the $3000. A few things may happen. The price of the furniture may go down, or you may find a better deal somewhere else. Either way you would save money by not paying the interest on a $3000 loan.

11) Think, think, think. Before buying anything, think about if you really need it. Think about if the money is needed somewhere else. And think if you can live without it.

12) If you must read a certain magazine, get a subscription. Most magazines that cost $4.99 for one, cost under $20 for a full year's subscription. Paying $4.99 for 12 months equals $59.88.

13) Cancel subscription and memberships that you are not using. Movie rental subscriptions, gym memberships, social club memberships, etc... Put that money somewhere it can be used.

Now to sum up what we have gone over in this chapter thus far let's looks at what I call The Tale of Two Moms. Mom one, we will call Jess and mom two we will call Pam. Now this tale is fiction, though very realistic in substance. Go get your calculator. This exercise is to show how proper money management and not-so-proper money management makes a big financial difference in the long run.

Jess and Pam stay in the same city; they both have an 11 year old son. To add another similarity, they both make $34,400 a year.

Jess	Expense	Pam
$625 rent	Housing per month	$650 mortgage
$250	Car note per month	$0
$90 per pair	Kid's shoes 5 per year	$40 per pair
$200	Groceries 12 times per year	$175
$250	Eating out per month	$80
$0	Savings per month	$150
$125	Utilities per month	$125
$95	Phone per month	$50
$85	Monthly budget leaks	$0

After looking over the chart above, what stands out to you about the spending habits of Jess?

After looking over the chart above, what stands out to you about the spending habits of Pam?

Continuing the story, let's look deeper into the money management of the two moms. Jess buys lunch each day at work, while Pam brings her lunch from home. Jess buys two entertainment magazines a month to read, which cost her $10.90 a month ($130.80 a year). Pam also reads two magazines a month. Pam reads money magazines and has a subscription to both, costing her $30 a year. Both moms are reading the same amount of magazines, yet Pam is spending $100 less. Pam saved a few extra dollars each month and paid cash for a nice used car. Jess did not want to wait, so she went and got her a car from a Buy Here Pay Here for $250 a month. Because Jess is financing her car, the car insurance payment is more. Pam is paying $25 more a month for housing, yet she owns her home. Pam plans to get a reverse mortgage on her house to supplement her retirement and SSI in her later years of life. A reverse mortgage is not an option for Jess because she is paying rent.

Each mom buys their son five pairs of shoes a year. Jess buys her son brand name shoes from the mall each time he needs a pair of shoes. Pam also buys her son brand name shoes. However, Pam shops in the discount section of the same store Jess gets her son's shoes from. Other times Pam goes to the outlet mall and gets the same shoes that Jess buys but for half the price. Pam uses coupons and buys discounted meat and freezes it. Pam prefers to cook and save money, as well as making healthy meals for her and her son. Jess has the latest cell phone with all the newest features. Pam on the other hand gets the same features as Jess; however Pam shopped around for the best deal. Pam is saving $150 a month ($1800 a year) for hard times. Jess on the other hand is saving zero a month. What will Jess do if an emergency comes up?

The last difference which is not listed is that Jess and Pam each get an income tax check. Many in today's society spend their income tax check. What do you think the two moms would do if they were to get a $2150 income tax return? There is no right or wrong answer.

Jess –

Pam –

My wife and I do know a teacher by the name of Ms. Harris who gets an income tax return check each year. Instead of spending the check, she puts the check in her savings account and the money gains interest. She told my wife that the money is extra and is not a part of her monthly budget. For as long as my wife and I have known her Ms. Harris has been doing this. My question to you: If you saved 5 years' worth of income tax checks and never spent them, what could you do with the money that you saved?

Write answer here.

I would like to branch off for a minute to converse about some businesses that are holding many people back from achieving financial increase. These businesses offer a service of sort, yet they tap into the "right now" mentality that has brainwashed so many people. Get those calculators back out, because this math is never good for the customer, only for the business.

The first type of business I wish for you to stay away from is Payday Loans/Cash Advance. What could be wrong with getting a short-term loan to get to your next paycheck? The easy answer is nothing. However, not many people pay off these loans in the 30 day repayment period. So how does this really work? Let's say John needs a loan to get to his next payday and goes to Big G Payday Loans to get a $400 loan. John writes Big G Payday Loans a check for $400 dollars. John is told that as long as he pays the loan back in full within 30 days, then there is no interest. Well when the 30th day comes, John goes in and states that he does not have the $400 in full. So, being the kind businesspeople that they are, the workers at Big G tell John that he only has to pay the interest, which is only 425% annually. That is a total annual interest amount of $1700. Divide that by 12 and you get a monthly interest payment of $141.67. Do you see where this is going? John pays the $141.67, and when he gets his receipt it states that his balance is now $400. Why? Because John only paid the interest and nothing on the principle amount that he borrowed. There are 3 different ways to pay off a Payday loan. First, pay it off in full. Second, pay the monthly interest payment, and whatever extra you pay then goes to the principle. Using this method, by paying just $50 more than the monthly interest payment it will take over half a year to pay the loan back. Just imagine paying back over $1100 for a $400 loan. The third way which many people do not know about is paying 4 equal payments to pay the loan off. But wait, there is a catch. This plan only happens when the loan company sees that you cannot pay back the loan in full (usually after you have paid 5 or more interest only payments). Then they will offer you the 4 equal payment options. By that time on a $400 loan you would have paid $708.35 in just interest. Another way to get a loan without writing a check is to let the loan company get your bank account and routing number. Yes, people actually give these businesses their bank account information and permission to withdraw from the account electronically. The average Payday Loan operation makes over $1.7 million a year.

The second type of business to stay away from is Title Pawns. A title pawn works just like a payday loan when it comes to interest rates and repayment practices. However, let's say John decided to pawn his car title instead of getting a payday loan. The worker at Big R Title Pawn gives John a $1500 loan on his car. Well, John knows that he can pay the loan off within his 30-day interest free period and is happy to hand his car title over. Along with the title to his car, John must also give them a copy of the key to the car. John gets the money and spends it on what it was intended for and other things. When the 30 days come he does not have the full amount and decided to pay the interest along with a few extra dollars to go toward the principle amount. Question: What happens if John cannot pay the loan back? Well that's where it gets interesting. Let's say John has paid 4 monthly interest payments – which equal a little over $2000 – and then cannot pay the loan off. Big R Title Pawn can then repossess John's car. And since he still owes them $1200 on the loan, they put a FOR SALE sign on his car in their car lot for $2200. Why is this? Title pawn companies will never loan out what the car is actually worth, but they will price the car for sale at the current value of the car. So in this case, Big R loaned out $1500, earned $2000 in interest, plus the $300 in principle that John Paid, and then sold the repossessed car for $2200. They netted a $3300 profit from just John. One title-pawn company for sale stated in its FOR SALE description a $7 million annual profit.

Across the country the repayment plan on title pawns vary by state. Like payday loans, repayments on title pawns can be paid by lump sum or installment. Some states, like North Carolina, do not allow title pawns at all.

The third type of business to stay far away from is Rent-to-Own businesses. This is the one that gets people who can't wait to own a television, furniture, jewelry, appliances, or a bedroom set. How does this work? Let's say John wants a living room set with tables and two lamps. He goes to the local rent-to-own and agrees to have the living room set delivered. The price is $2500. The weekly (yes weekly) payments are $48.08 for twenty four months. Get your calculator and multiply that out. Twenty four months multiplied by $48.08 is... hold on. The agreement said weekly. $48.08 multiplied by 104 payments is $5000.32. That's a mighty big difference. Well, the payment of $48.08 goes to two different directions. Half of the payment goes to the rental fee, and the other half goes towards owning the item or items. So for every $48.08 that John pays, $24.04 goes to the $2500 that the items were advertised for. And by the time that he is done paying, he could have bought the same living room set two times.

When a person cannot wait to get something, these are the places they go to get what they want right then. What would it hurt to wait just a few more days for an item? Just think, if John would put that same $48.08 in the bank in a savings account on that same weekly basis, he would have $5000.32 saved. The only difference is that the bank would have paid him interest on the money. If John was in a financial bind before getting the payday and/or title loan, just imagine how much of a financial bind he is in having to pay those high rates back every month. How much financial logic does that make?

None of these businesses are in business to help its customers create wealth. How could they be if they are legally robbing the customer of their hard earned money? However, all of the blame is not on the businesses, the customers are to blame for these businesses staying open.

What else could John have done instead of going to a payday loan?

What else could John have done before going to a title pawn?

What else could John have done instead of going to a rent-to-own?

Let's now talk about a subject that many people do not like to talk about: debt. By definition debt is something owed: an amount of money, a service, or an item of property that is owed to somebody. Debt is counteractive to being an opportunistic millionaire. No matter how much debt you have, you should plan with all your power to get your overall debt to a zero balance. How would you feel after obtaining a bank account with one million dollars just to get phone calls from and letters stating that you are being sued for outstanding debt? Just as you should pay all of your bills on time to avoid late fees, you should pay off all your debt to avoid future financial headache. I must stress that while paying off debt one should not create new bills. Do not add a car note. Do not agree to anything that would cause you to pay a monthly fee. Do not join any memberships.

There are many article online, books you can buy, and programs to get to show you how to get out of debt. Well I'm going to simplify the process for you by telling you what my wife and I did. First, we gathered all of our bills and put them in a three-ring binder. Each bill got its own plastic sleeve. On a note card I wrote down the name of the bill and the amount owed, and then placed the note card in the sleeve with the corresponding bill. Next, we did something that many people would call extreme: we called the bill collectors and the companies that we owed. During the call we would ask what they would take as a payoff amount. For instance if we owed a company $340, they may take $200 as a payoff and settle the debt. We would then ask them to send a bill stating the agreement and we would send them a money order upon getting the bill. We put in our budget $400 a month to pay off all outstanding debt.

At the first of each month, we sent off $400 in money orders to pay off our debt. You may not have $400 to pay toward your bills each month. However, pick a dollar amount that you can manage and start there. No matter if it's only $100 (or even $5) a month, start somewhere. It may take a year, or maybe five years depending on your debt and amount you pay, but it's all worth it. Create for yourself a long-term goal and something to work toward. Our goal was the fact that we did not want anything hindrance on our credit in the process of purchasing our first four-plex.

Understand, you are in control of what happens in your life. You are the only part of your life equation that you have 100% control. Control your debt. Control your finances. And control your life. There are two words that must go through your head: budget and plan. As long as you have a budget and a plan then you can do whatever you want financially. Once you have paid off all of your debt, do not spend the extra money you are going to have. If you are in deep debt, do not get a debt consolidation loan. Why would you get a company to pay your bills for you? The company has to make money as well, and they are going to make their money from you. It is counterproductive to pay a company to do something that you can do yourself.

Let me tell you about Wendy. Wendy had no debt and decided to buy a new living room set. However she decided to finance the new furniture for 24 months. Wendy set down after the furniture arrived and realized that she didn't want to be paying for the furniture for two years and developed a plan. Wendy got a part-time job. She then took every dollar that she made at her second job and put the entire check to paying off the balance of the furniture. Wendy was not deep in debt, but what she did could be used as a way to pay off any outstanding balance that one may have.

End of chapter thoughts

Would you rather look like a million dollars or have a million dollars in the bank? Explain your answer

What can a $115 pair of basketball shoes do for you that a $50 pair of basketball shoes made by the same company can't do?

Name 5 things you can do differently right now with your finances.
1

2

3

4

5

Chapter 7 – What's Your Number?

First let me start off by saying that the name of this book is Opportunistic Millionaire. Yet, everyone does not need a million dollars to be happy. Everyone does not desire to be a millionaire; rather they choose to want to live comfortably. Now to the question: What is your number?

For me personally, I have a few numbers. Looking at the current real-estate market I can buy a four-plex for $150,000. With that four-plex my family could stay in one of the units and rent out the other 3 units in the four-plex. After that I would buy another four-plex. Thus, I would then add another $150,000 to the original amount. Once that it done, I will then add the cost of a house for my family. In the current market where we want to live a nice 3 to 4 bedroom house with a few acres would cost us around $170,000. Our overall number would be $470,000. Once again, yes the name of this book is Opportunistic Millionaire. In the area where we want our four-plexes we could rent our units for $700 to $900 a month. If there is no mortgage, where would the income from the rental units go to? The answer: working our way to being a millionaire. On paper this looks and sounds very simple. I already know that some tenants are going to be short on rent some months. There will be months were there may be more than one vacant unit. Repairs will come up and things will need to be replaced. However, I know that this will take hard work and determination. Yes, hard work and determination. I know for a fact that the road to where I am determined to get will not be easy. However nothing easy is worth having. And if it were that easy everyone would do it.

What is your number? What is the amount of money that you need in the bank? What could you be doing right now to get yourself to that number? What would you do once you get to that number?

Ben and his wife Janet both make descent incomes, yet Ben would like for he and his wife to retire early. To retire early Ben figures they will need an extra $30,000 in the bank. Ben writes out a plan and shows it to Janet. They agree that the plan is attainable and starts putting the plan in motion to put an extra $30,000 in the bank. They take a look at their spending. In their current budget they allotted $200 a month for eating out. The decided they would save that money and cut eating out down to just once a month. Janet added that she would stop buying her morning coffee and opts to get a reusable sealable cup and make coffee at home, and put that money into a new savings account which they name Goal30. Those were the small things that the couple did. They then cleaned out their home of all the items they did not want or use, and had a yard sale. Ben and Janet watched their spending and any time they could put a few extra dollars in their Goal30 account they did. The two stopped drinking sodas and opted to drink water (which was a healthy choice as well). It took Ben and Janet 3 ½ years to reach their goal. Which was longer than their projected 2 ½ year plan, but most importantly they reached the goal. They didn't give up, and they stayed focus on their goal.

Let's work on how to get to that number.
1) First, do you want to buy a house or pay rent? Would you want to buy a house, condo, or townhome? Do you want to buy a mini farm and make extra money?
2) How much debt do you need to pay off before you have no old bills? Do you need a debt management plan as well as a budget plan?
3) What expenses will you have once you reach your number? Will these expenses cause your number to go up?
4) What are your annual expenses? What are your monthly expenses? What are your weekly expenses?
5) How much will you have in your emergency fund? What do you consider an emergency?
6) How much do you expect to get from Social Security? Could this amount make your number go up or down?

7) What all do you want? What size house? What kind of car? What type of clothes? Do you want a pet? These questions must be answered to get you to your number.

8) Look forward at what may come up. Birthdays, holidays, repairs, etc...

9) And once you think you have a number, add 10% to that total, just to be safe.

Get the calculator and sit down.

End of chapter thoughts

What is your number?

Are you willing to work hard to reach this number?

To reach your goal, what are you willing to give up?

Are you ready to think differently to attain your goal?

How will you think differently?

Chapter 8 – Fill in the Blank

As if you haven't been filling in enough information already, here is more. The difference now is the following questions are the beginning of you being an opportunistic millionaire, and getting to where you want to be financially. Below are a series of questions for you to answer. There are no wrong answers, only your answers. Please refer back to these answers over time and adjust them accordingly as needed.

What is your financial goal for the next...
1 month –

3 months –

6 months –

1 year –

3 years –

5 years –

What steps must you take to reach your goals in the next...

1 month –

3 months –

6 months –

1 year –

3 years –

5 years –

What setbacks do you foresee in attaining your goals in the next...

1 month –

3 months –

6 months –

1 year –

3 years –

5 years –

What steps will you take when setbacks interfere with your plans?

What does retire mean to you?

At what age do you want to retire?

What will be your expenses once you retire?

What will be your income once you retire?

How much do you need in your emergency fund?

End of chapter thoughts
Write down what each statement means to you.

You can do anything; make sure it's something you enjoy.

The only part of any life equation that you can change is you. And once you change the equation changes. And once the equation changes the outcome changes.

Let nothing stop you from getting what you need to get where you want to be.

Never give up on a dream that you know is attainable.

Chapter 9 – Start-Ups: A Few Ideas

Listed in this chapter are businesses an individual can start to make extra income or to work full time. NOTE: Always follow all local and federal laws when starting a business. However, before we get to the list of businesses that one can start, let's look at the minimum cost of starting a business. If you are starting a business from home you will need these basic items: business license, business cards, and a web site. In most areas of the country a business license cost $200 or less. There are numerous companies that make business cards. One online company sells 250 business cards for $10. So right now we are at $210. Now a website. There are many avenues that can be taken when setting up a website. Some online companies offer free websites if you add their name to your web address. However, you can get a website for around $40 a year. So, there we are a total of $250.

I personally suggest that you find a business that you will enjoy. Please do not start a business just to make massive amounts of money. Make massive amounts of money so that you can live the life you want. It is said that people who enjoy their job never actually work. Again, start a business that you will enjoy, and it will never feel like you were working.

Businesses that can be started for under $500

Accessory Business
Do you like making jewelry? How about scarfs? Are you good at sewing and knitting? What do you think about making baby burp clothes? This is a great business for someone who wants to own their own business and keep the creative juices flowing all at the same time.

Computer Tutor
If you are an expert at Windows or Linux, desktop publishing or Web research, HTML or word processing, you have the skills to help

others learn how to work and operate a computer. Many older citizens do not know how to properly operate a computer or tablet and would pay to have someone help them. You could use your computer or theirs.

DJ Service

Do you like people and music? This may be the option for you. Good DJs are still in demand. DJs are needed for birthdays, anniversaries, weddings, office parties, dances, as well as holiday events. You must have a large selection of music to cover all kinds of music lovers and backgrounds. Getting quality sound equipment that is portable and easy to hookup is a plus. Many customers will come from previous events, so do a good job. Many DJs charge a flat fee, others charge per job. There are a few that charge by the hour. Whatever the case, this is a great way to bring in an extra $300 or more a weekend.

Editorial Service

Many people want to have their book published, but have no clue how to properly examine their own work and turn a manuscript into a ready-to-publish book. Editorial services help with editing, proofing, copy editing, book doctoring, and indexing among other things. This business can be done out of a spare bedroom. This service could also be extended to those who are writing thesis and dissertations.

Event and Party Planner

Just as the first business listed above, being an event planner could be a full time business or be done on the side for extra income. If you have an outgoing personality and are organized this may be the business for you. Get some business cards. Introduce yourself to various venues, DJs, florists, caterers, photographers, and limo services. Many event planners charge a percentage of the budget. Others charge a flat rate per event. Best of all, this business can be done out of the comfort of your home.

Got Land?

This one heading alone could be a book in and of itself. There are so many ways that one can make a reasonable income if they have land.

- Raise small animals such as chicken, rabbits, and quails.
- Grow herbs, vegetables, and fruit. Selling these items will not only make money but it would save money by not having to buy the items in the grocery store.
- There are those who also raise worms on their land. This can be done on a small area (even in a storage tote).
- Raising honey could also be an idea as long as the person isn't scared of or allergic to bees.
- If a person has enough land and a few animals, starting a petting zoo on the land would be a great idea.
- Open an outdoor gun/archery range would be great if someone has the patience to go through the licensing process and have the necessary training this idea could be very lucrative.

Home Cleaning Service

What if you had 20 clients paying you $50 a week to come to their house for 2 hours a week to do some cleaning? That would be $1000 a week, or $52,000 a year. Items needed would include regular household cleaning supplies, some company shirts, and some business cards. You will make the decision on what you are willing to do. Make sure your customers know this before you get started cleaning. Get some simple agreements made so that both parties know exactly what will be cleaned and on what days. If a good job is done, word-of-mouth referral will start flooding your phone.

Item Flipper

Item flipping is like many other businesses, you get out of it what you put into it. How does this work? Go to yard sales, thrift stores, or pick up items from the side of the road, then resell the items. Having a good eye for knowing what is good and can be resold for profit is a plus. Selling the items on craigslist or on collectors' web sites will generate your customer base. There is a YouTube video showing Tristen O'Brian buying items from various Goodwill stores in one day and making over $1000 in profit after selling the items. Another item flipper, Aaron LaPedis wrote a book about flipping items. LaPedis has made over a million dollars flipping items.

Lawn Care Service
If you already have every piece of lawn care equipment imaginable then starting this business would be a no brainer. If you do not own the proper equipment already, then starting this business for under $500 is still achievable if you buy used equipment. You do the math. How many customers do you want to have? Now multiply that number by the average cost of service. The only downfall is there may not be any work from mid-November to late February in some parts of the US. However, this time could be used to offer leaf pickup or snow removal services. Most lawn care owners start pricing at $35 per yard. Using the bottom rate, if you have 20 customers a week your weekly income will be $700.

Laundry Service
Since many people dread doing laundry and still need to get it done this will be a great business to start. Advertise to working couples and singles. Pick up their laundry and have it ready before they get home from work. Or offer next day service. Either way you would be offering them a service so that they could have more free time after they get off from a long day of work. Also, looking into doing laundry service at large apartment complexes would also be a great place to generate clientele. Prices are set by charging an hourly rate on top of the per load fee.

MaryKay or Avon Independent Sales Representative
This could be a side gig or a full time job depending on how much effort a person wants to put into the business. Not only do sales reps show products out of brochures, now the rep can also opt for

an online store. Rep fee, business cards, brochures, a car magnet, and the total cost are still less than $150.

Mobile Auto Tune-Up Service

If you do not mind getting dirty and know your way around a car this may be the job for you. Every car will need a tune-up at some point and time. Why not make the money tuning up vehicles? You will need the proper tools, business cards, and maybe the spark plugs and wires for some jobs. You could do the job at customer's homes or at their place of employment. If you purchase the sparkplugs and wires, make sure you get a customer rewards card from your auto parts store. Doing this will generate deals and discounts for you when making future purchases. This business could evolve to a mobile auto mechanic service.

Mobile Car Wash and Detailing

This is a great business to get out of the house. With your basic car cleaning supplies and a hand held vacuum you have all you need to start a mobile car wash and detailing business. I saw a mobile car wash and detail business owner outside of my office building in Charlotte. He was called by one customer to come to the building to do one car. While doing that car others saw him and hired him to do their cars as well.

Mobile Window Tint

With some training and the basic equipment needed, you can start your own window-tinting business. This business could evolve from tinting just automobiles to homes, high-rise condominiums and office buildings. Make sure you learn local ordinances for vehicle tint before starting this business.

Music Lessons

So many people want to learn how to play an instrument. If you have the ability and the patience to teach others how to play this would be a great business to start. To start this business, one would need time, space, and business cards. The client would have their own instrument. Services could also be provided to those who do not have instruments if the business owner has instruments the clients can use. Note: We were paying $12 for 30-minute guitar lessons for our son.

Online Book Store

Own and operate your own book store from home. Books can be sold on Amazon, eBay, and other web sites. Books can be bought at various locations and resold for a profit. Like most businesses, you will only get out of this business what you put in. One online book store owner reported making $40,000 a year.

Personal Athletic Coach

Many parents want the best for their kids. A personal coach is someone the parents can hire to help their child improve in a particular sport. This would be a great business to start for anyone who was a former college athlete or anyone who already coaches to make extra income in the offseason.

Seminar Promotion

People love information. If you are good at promoting events and connecting people, this may be the business for you to start. You can bring in life coaches, medical specialist, and authors. You can charge at the door or take a percentage of what the speaker makes. This can also be used to host How-To classes to help others generate clientele.

Tutor

Are you good in an academic subject that many have problems with? Can you guide students in the right direction in a particular subject? Answer yes to those two questions and this may be the extra income job for you. As a tutor you would help kids do better in school or prepare teens for standardized tests. Tutors usually charge $10 to $25 an hour.

Other Businesses that can be started for under $500.
Airbrush Artist
Boat Cleaning Service
Clown/Magician Service
Hauling Service
Hiking Guide
Mobile Dog Groomer
Mobile Hair Hairstylist/ Barber
Personal Shopper
Pet Sitter
Reminder Service

iamShawnOusley.com

Always have your
business card ready.

Businesses that can be started for under $5000

Car Wash
This by far is a very simple business to start and all it takes is a good location some water and proper car cleaning supplies. Depending on where you are located, the weather may give you almost year-round availability. I have personally seen a guy start a car washing/cleaning business next to a gas station whose automatic car wash malfunctioned. Remember, most people want to drive a clean car, and if you do a great job word will get out and repeat business will follow.

Clean Out Service
When people move out of a house or apartment, they usually leave a mess creating a need for a clean out service. The clean out service takes out all of the furniture, garbage, clothes, etc... that is left behind by the previous dwellers and haul it off to the dump. Also included would be cleaning the floors and walls and sweeping out the house. Additional services can be added for a charge to the home owner. If you are thinking as an opportunistic millionaire, the items removed could also be resold at a yard sale, a flea market, or on craigslist.

Hotdog Cart Stand
The cost of a used cart can cost as little as $200. If going with a new cart is more your style, it can cost as much as $5500. Many hotdog vendors work less than 5 hours a day and bank over $70,000 a year. Having a good product is the key with this business. The vendor should have turkey hotdogs as well as beef hotdogs, all of the toppings, and a selection of chips. As for beverages, bottled water and a selection of sodas would be sufficient.

Mobile Auto Repair
Just like the mobile auto tune-up service, but on a larger scale. Many mechanics have chosen to stop working for someone else and start working for themselves instead. Mobile mechanics with

the proper equipment can make as much as $500 a day depending on the services they offer. Doing the math, $500 a day for 5 days is $2500 a week (working five days a week and off two). The customers can purchase required parts or you can. Be reminded, you may want to buy the parts if you get customer reward points from a parts store. Many mobile mechanics advertise on craigslist and get many referrals by word of mouth. As long as you do a good job and have fair prices there will never be a shortage of work.

Mover

Movers are always needed. Many cities that have colleges have a yearly turnover rate. What does this mean to a mover? This means that you could possibly move a customer in, and in less than a year move the same customer out. Many apartment complexes also have high turnover, which would also be a great place to generate customers. An enclosed truck would be the best vehicle to use in this business. Also an extra set of hands to move that wood furniture helps. Customers can be charged by the hour, by the move, or per load depending on what is being moved and how far. One large moving franchise charges $30 per hour from the time they leave their office until the time they return to their office. Needed items would consist of a moving truck, hand dolly, wrapping blankets, business cards, and employee t-shirts.

Vending Machine Owner

Vending machines can cost as much as $3000 for one. Others can be bought used. Placement is the most important part of starting a vending machine company. Usually, vending machines are placed in places where there are at least 30 people a day in the building/office where the machine is placed. This business will work best if you have two or more vending machines. Bubble gum machines start off around $120; take $15 to fill up, and nets around $125 when emptied. Today vending machines are not limited to just snacks and soda. Think opportunistically and decide where the best place to sell what item.

Other Businesses that can be started for under $5000.
Massage Therapist
Pig Farmer
Private Investigator
Taxidermist
Virtual Assistant
Franchises that can be started for under $15,000

ALCO-BUDDY
This is a breathalyzer vending machine company.
Fee: $2000 & up

Building Stars
This is a commercial cleaning franchise. Building Stars offer a step-by-step training program. Franchise Fee: $1900

Clean & Happy Windows
Founded in 1990 and began franchising in 2000, this is an opportunity to start a low entry cost window cleaning franchise. Franchise Fee: $100-$2000

Cruise One
This is a travel agency with concentration in cruises.
Franchise Fee: $10,000

Discount Clipper
This is a direct mail coupon company. Franchise Fee: $1000

KC Home Inventory
Ideal for someone who may want to start slow and run a business part time and then grow it into a fulltime job. No annual franchise, affiliate or partnership fee. You keep all the profit. Franchise Fee: $195-$425

Sniferz

This is a deodorizing and air purification franchise opportunity. Franchise Fee: $6500

Southhill Designs
My wife actually does this and loves it. Design and sell your own jewelry. This company is always coming out with new products. Shameless plug: southhilldesigns.com/lakeeshaousley. Franchise Fee: $59-$199

Status Business Solutions
This is your opportunity to own your commercial cleaning business. Franchise Fee: $3,500 and up

Stretch-n-Grow International
Fitness program for kids ages 3-8. The program covers health, nutrition, and sports. Franchise Fee: $10,000

Tropical Flavored Shake
This business comes with no annual franchise or royalty fees. You receive all you need to start your business, plus support and assistance with getting started.
Franchise Fee: $1300

Weiss Publishing Group
This is a business consulting franchise opportunity.
Franchise Fee: $249

Whitening on Wheels
This is a teeth-whitening business opportunity. The company states that this is not a franchise, you will own the business.
Fee: $59 - $3729

End of chapter thoughts

What type of business would you like to start?

Are you happy with your current job?

Would you be happier doing what you love, yet only making 85% of what you make now?

Do you believe that hard work pays off in the long run?

What does the following statement means to you?
When you are stuck between a rock and a hard place, keep moving forward.

Chapter 10 – What's Stopping You? / Get Motivated

Motivation, drive, determination, and inspiration are words that many people use to describe how they got to where they are in life. What motivates a person to work 12 to 16-hour days for their own business? The answer: Their goals, willingness to achieve, and desire to succeed. Despair, defeat, beat, and hopelessness are words that people who give up use. They never achieve what they could have because they let an obstacle block the vision of their goal.

Did you know that many people failed before being successful? The average millionaire has more than 15 failed attempts before they finally discover what actually works for them. Regardless of how many times they fail or are rejected they did not give up. We have all heard the statement, "It's not how many times you fall that matters; it's how many times you get up." My question to you is how many times can you take rejection or failure before giving up?

The author of the Harry Potter series, J.K. Rowling, was turned down by multiple publishers over many years before being able to publish the first Harry Potter book. Henry Ford, the founder of Ford Motor Company, went broke five times because of failed businesses before starting the car company. Howard Schultz the founder of Starbucks was turned down by over 240 banks. Hank Aaron went 0 for 5 when he started playing professional baseball with the Milwaukee Braves. Dr. Seuss's first book was rejected by 27 publishers. Yep, Dr. Seuss, rejected.

Now, Harry Potter is a multi-billion dollar industry with movies, books toys, and games. What would have happened if J.K. Rowling would have given up on her dream? If Howard Schultz would have given up, where would people stop in the morning to get their morning cup of coffee? What if Hank Aaron decided that baseball really wasn't for him after going 0 for 5 his first time stepping up to a major league plate? What rhythmic rhyming books would kids read if there were no green eggs & ham, or a cat in a hat? Now, no kid's book collection is complete without at least one Dr. Seuss book.

There is nothing that can stop a person from achieving their goals but themselves. People who succeed have learned that obstacles will come up. However, how a person deals with those obstacles is the difference between succeeding and giving up. Money low? Keep moving forward. Car broke? Keep moving forward. No inventory? Keep moving forward? No matter what, keep moving forward.

There's a big difference between someone who wakes up and says "I'm going to try to succeed" and the person who says "I'm going to succeed."

Knowing that nothing will stop you from reaching your goal is what makes or breaks an opportunistic millionaire. If your cash gets low and you have a goal, decide on what you can do to reach that goal without money. Making phone calls and following up with previous customers may be the plan for that day. Writing out a plan for a new marketing strategy would be wise. If your car breaks down, then decide what you can do to reach clients without driving. Maybe door-to-door marketing in the neighborhood is a good idea that day. There is always something that can be done for you to reach your goals. Kent, the lawn care business owner stated that on rainy days he cleans his equipment. After cleaning the equipment he goes out and speaks with business owners about their lawn care. He said that even on off days there is some work that can be done.

There's a saying that says everyone wants to go to heaven but nobody wants to die. Well, everybody wants to be a millionaire, but everyone will not work hard to get there. When a person's mindset changes, then the outcome will change for that person. Doing nothing to get somewhere actually gets a person nowhere. Doing something to get somewhere, will indeed get you somewhere. Thus, do something and let nothing stop you. Think about how many people you know that make claims about what they are going to do when they get X amount of money. Now ask yourself, what that person is doing to get there. Now think of a person you know that you consider successful. What did that person do to get to where they are?

Whatever it takes to motivate you to reach your goals use it to the fullest. If you need a motivational quote each day, sign up for a daily motivational text or e-mail. If there is a house or car you want, take a picture and keep it in your pocket or set the picture somewhere that you have no choice but to see it each day. Do you want to set aside money for your kids? Just think about them when you are working on achieving your goals. Accept responsibility for those few failures you may have, but learn from those failures and keep moving forward.

Keep a "To-Do" list and a daily journal. This will help you keep your focus on what is important to you. If you have daily goals to reach, you will have a joy knowing that you accomplished a goal at the end of the day. Each time you reach your monthly goals you will have a greater joy within yourself. And joy is a great thing to have when working toward a life goal.

To achieve your goals, sacrifice must be made. You have to be eager to move forward no matter what, stay determined, and stay motivated. When barriers occur that might hinder the ordinary person, you stay the course because staying the course is your only option. There will be sacrifice. There will be setbacks. But at the place when others would give up, you rise and take on the challenge. You will achieve your goals. You will achieve everything you set your mind to. You are the only thing that can stop you. You will be great at what you do, because you have decided that where you want to be is more important than where you are now. When you get there, you will know that you have succeeded. Once you have succeeded there will be the moment when you look back and realize that you created your own path, and that is a moment worth working toward.

Write down if you agree or disagree with the following statement and explain why or why not.

Successful people read every day, while unsuccessful people watch television every day.

A successful person wants others to succeed, while an unsuccessful person secretly wishes for other to fail.

Successful people rise above excuses, while unsuccessful people make excuses.

A person can be motivated in many ways. To this day, football teams across the country still watch "Rudy" on game day. Why? The movie "Rudy" shows how an undersized football player worked hard to achieve his dream of playing football for Notre Dame. However, everyone is not a football player. Thus, others are motivated through songs. "The Impossible Dream" is a song that inspires individuals to strive to reach their dreams. Personally, I love quotes.

On any given day I will read or think of one of the many quotes that keeps me going. Let me share with you a few of the quotes.

> It's never too late to be what you might have been.
> – George Elliot

The true test of a man is how he treats someone who can do him absolutely no good. -- Samuel Johnson

If it is to be it is up to me. – Unknown

You can't get steak dinner outcomes with peanut butter & jelly work ethic. – Shawn Ousley

What motivates you? Does the vision of you working for yourself and not having to answer to a supervisor motivation to you? Does knowing that you can earn more income working for yourself motivate you? Making a financially secure future for your kids, is that your motivation? The dream of retiring early motivates many. Motivation by definition is the act of giving somebody a reason or incentive to do something. The definition continues – a reason for doing something or behaving in a particular way. I guess the title of this book could have been The Motivated Millionaire, but I personally was fond of the word opportunistic.

I challenge you to write down your goals and what motivates you to achieve those goals. Write your goals on three sheets of paper. Hang those sheets of paper on the walls in your home. Make sure you see that sheet every day. Hang one sheet by the bathroom mirror. Hang one sheet next to your dresser. Hang the third sheet of paper on the refrigerator. Research shows that when a person writes down and sees their goals they are more likely to achieve their goals.

After you write those goals down, on another sheet of paper write down what you want. Everyone has a dream car or a dream house. Go to a car dealership and take an up close look at that dream car. If you are really feeling great, take it for a test drive. Know what it feels like to drive your dream car. Next go to an open house (usually on a Sunday), and see what your dream house looks like up close and in person. That may be the instant motivation that you may need. Keep in mind the feeling you have when you are looking at your dream car. Think about the smell and look of the car's interior. Remember the sound system. Recall what it was like to walk into that home. Each time you feel like giving up and throwing in the towel remember what your dream looks like, what it smells like, and what it feels like.

Let me tell you what my household did. We found pictures of everything we wanted: house with land to start a mini farm, certain types of vehicles, animals, 4-plexes, etc... and then put all of the pictures on one sheet and made copies to hang up throughout our apartment. Less than 3 months later we closed on our house with land. Next, we got a few animals. Yes we changed our focus and decided to buy a house first and then get a 4-plex. The point is if you see your goals and dreams you will have no choice but to focus on achieving those goals and dreams.

My motivational speech to you.

No one has gotten anywhere by sitting still. Choose on this day to be somebody. Not just anybody, but the person you see yourself to be. Be the person you want to be. You have the power within you to change the flavor of your day. You have the power within you to change the flavor of your week. You, have the power within you to change the flavor of your life. Wake up every morning and say to yourself, "Today is the day that I get one step closer to my dream. Today is the day that I get one step closer to my goal. Someday is today, and not some future date. The future is now, and I will not wait for someone to hand me my dream. I will create my own path." No barrier can stop you, no setback will halt your progress, you will stay determined, and you will stay the course. With every heartbeat, every breath, and with each step you take. Nothing can stand in the way of a person who is determined. I challenge you to stay determined. Leave all negativity in the past. Stay away from those who discourage you. Block out all negative people. This is a new day, old habits are no more, and you are a new person – a new person who is focused. Encourage yourself at all times. Can't is a word for those who make excuses. Excuses keep you from achieving. Excuses give you a reason to quit, and you are not a quitter. You have a dream to achieve, a dream to make true, you are driven to succeed. Nothing can hinder you from getting to where you have destined yourself to be.

Shawn Ousley

End of chapter thoughts

What motivates you?

Chapter 11 – V.I.S.I.O.N.

Merriam-Webster gives three definitions of vision:
1) the ability to see : sight or eyesight
2) something that you imagine : a picture that you see in your mind
3) something that you see or dream

All are accurate definitions. In becoming an opportunistic millionaire you want to focus on the second definition. You have to see where you want to go; you have to have an image in your head of your goal. Make the ʳ vision detailed and shaped just for you.

Added to the definitions provided by Merriam-Webster, left break down VISION so that it gives you an in-depth focus to achieving your goals and dreams that you set for yourself.

V – Visualize

Each day visualize your goals. Know where you want to go and where you want to be.

I – Instructions

Write out a list of everything you need to do to achieve your goals. These are your instructions. Once this list is done, then do something every single day on the list. At all times continue to move forward.

S – See It

Look at your list every day. Seeing your list will engrave the instructions in your mind. This will also keep you focused on the task at hand.

I – Incorporate

Incorporate reading, learning, and asking. The reason: Read Chapter 4.

O – Opportunity

As stated in Chapter 3, keep your eyes and ears open because opportunity is everywhere.

N - Now

Now is the time. The right time to start your path to success is now. Not tomorrow. Not when the things are right. Now is the time.

Chapter 12 – Suggested Readings

Below is a suggested list of books that I feel will help you along your journey to becoming an opportunistic millionaire and achieving your financial goals. There are many books that I could put on this list. There are hundreds of books on making money, being a millionaire, self-confidence, and motivation. I have read so many that I have lost count. However, there are 3 books that I find myself always suggesting to individuals to read. Below is my very brief list of suggested readings. Enjoy.

1 – The Richest Man in Babylon
      by George Samuel Clason

2 – The Millionaire Next Door
      by Thomas J. Stanley

3 – Rich Dad, Poor Dad
      by Robert T. Kiyosaki

Chapter 13 – Forms

You have my permission to copy the pages of this chapter as many times as you need. This chapter consists of forms that you may want to utilize to accomplish the goals that you have set for yourself.

Bonus
E-mail Shawn@iamShawnOusley.com, type FORMS in the Subject line and get the forms in a pdf file.

Goals

Short-term Goals
Financial Goals to achieve within three years

Goal	Goal Date	Cost	Amount Saved or Paid	Amount to save per month

Mid-term Goals
Financial Goals to achieve within three to six years

Goal	Goal Date	Cost	Amount Saved or Paid	Amount to save per month

Long-term Goals
Financial Goals to achieve within six to ten years

Goal	Goal Date	Cost	Amount Saved or Paid	Amount to save per month

Record of Daily Spending

Write in what you spend for 1 month, make as many copies as needed.

Date →	1	2	3	4	5	6	7	8	9	10	Total
Item											
Gas for Car											
Cell Phone											
Vending Machine											
Baber Shop/Salon											
Utility Bills											
Tobacco/ Alcohol											
Childcare											
Coffee											
Groceries											
Food at Work											
Fast Food											

At the end of the month add up the totals and see where your money was spent. Write down every cent spent.

Assets and Liabilities

Assets	Dollar Amount		Liabilities	Dollar Amount
Cash in Hand			Car Loan	
Checking Account			Student Loan	
Savings Account			Credit Cards	
Car Value			Mortgage Balance	
Real Estate Value			State Taxes	
Personal Property			Federal Taxes	
Certificates of Deposits			Leases	
Bonds			Other Loans	
Stocks			Other	
Mutual Funds			Other	
IRA				
401(K)			Total Liabilities	$
Retirement Account				
Other				
Total Assets	$		Assets	$
			Minus Liabilities	$
			Equals Net Worth	$

On the next page you will find the Credit Dispute Form. I suggest that everyone gets a copy of their credit report every year and dispute all items on the report that are seen as false. When you dispute an item on the report make sure you write out the account number as it appears on the credit report. Only send a dispute to the credit bureau(s) that have the account listed. This may seem time consuming, but it is worth the time. You can dispute ownership of the account, amount stated on the account, identity theft, or false information. You can inform the bureaus that the account is not your account, the account was included in bankruptcy, was paid in full, or that a late payment was never made. You can go to www.annualcreditreport.com and get a free copy of your credit report. Be sure to get the proper mailing addresses to the three credit bureaus: Experian, Equifax, and TransUnion.

Credit Dispute

Name_____

Current Address _____

_____

Previous Address_____

_____

Social Security # ***-**-_____.

Company Name_____
Account Number_____
The reason I am disputing this account _____

_____
_____
_____
_____
_____
_____
_____
_____
_____
_____
_____
_____
_____
_____
_____
_____
_____
_____
_____
_____
_____
_____

Self-Contract For Achieving Goals

State exact goal: _____

Goal Date _____

I will know when I achieved my goal when _____

_____

This goal is important to me _____

_____

_____

_____

The steps to reach my goal are _____

_____

_____

The possible barriers that will prevent me from achieving my goals are _____

_____

_____

I will deal with barriers _____

_____

_____

_____

_____

I will overview my progress _____

_____

_____

The accomplishments along the way to ensure that my goal is reached are _____

_____

_____

To achieve my goal, each day I must _____

_____

_____

_____

_____

Chapter 14 – Three Blog Post

Why You Should Live Your Life Like It's Game Seven
by **Shawn Ousley**

GAME 7
No other words are more relevant in sports than those two words.

I remember hearing a commentator say "Big time players make big time plays in big time games." Well I am here to tell you that Game 7 is that big time game. It doesn't matter if it's the first round of the playoffs, the divisional round, The NBA Finals, The World Series, or the Stanley Cup Finals. If it's Game 7, then all bets are off. Game 7 is when pain is replaced by adrenaline. There are no excuses in Game 7. There are no "what ifs" in Game 7. There is no "Wait until next time" in Game 7, because that time is now. Game 7 has but one meaning: Win the game or go home. Game 7 will either end in victory or defeat. The winner of Game 7 either goes on to the next round or is crowned the champion.

I'm getting hype just typing this. Because something inside of me knows what Game 7 means. The neurological triggers in my mind are going crazy typing this because I am talking about Game 7.

Now, why should you live your life like it is Game 7? You want to live your life with excitement and enthusiasm.

You only get one life. You either win or not. That is up to you. Live life without "what ifs". What if you don't live you r life like it is Game 7? What if you wait until next time? What if next time doesn't come? This is your life. Not your parents' life. Your life. This is not a life for someone to live vicariously through you. It's your life. Your life is your Game 7.

You are the big time player in the big time game, and that game is your life. And it's your life to make those big time plays, meaning making moves and decisions to get you to where you want to be.

Someone hurt your feelings? Who cares? Get back in the game. You made a bad move? Shake it off and get back in the game. Lied on, talked about, misunderstood? Shake it off and get back in the game.

I'll tell you something else about Game 7, no one remembers the bad things that happen in Game 7. People remember the crowd erupting plays. Fans remember the winner. So no matter what happens in your life, as long as you bounce yourself back into your Game 7, no one will remember the bad.

So on this day, I ask you, I command of you: Live your life like it's Game 7.

Now if you are ready to live your life like it's Game 7, please allow me to help you. I guarantee, my book will help lead you in the right direction to get started. Click Here if you are ready to live your life like it is Game 7.

I am Shawn Ousley, Follow Your Passion / Follow Your Dream

Why I'm Glad My Niece Decided to be a Makeup Artist Instead of a Nurse

by **Shawn Ousley**

After graduating high school my niece set off to college to earn a degree in nursing. While in college her major changed to History. Then it changed again to undecided. After spending two semesters away from home and in college she came home for the summer and decided that she wanted to go to school to be a makeup artist. This information she held for a while from her mom and from me.

I learned of her decision from my wife. The next day I called my niece and informed her that I was with her in her decision.

She stated to me that she thought I would be upset and would disapprove of her wanting to go to a vocational type school for makeup artistry. I explained to her that I know that she loves makeup. I know that she would be happy if all she did was work with makeup each and every day.

I then went on to tell her that while she is still young and single she should pursue whatever makes her happy. I also explained to her that no matter what she does there is someone making a fortune doing it – whether it is in the medical field or doing makeup. Then I asked her why shouldn't she be the one making a fortune each year doing makeup.

As long as you are doing what you love, then it will never feel like working. The worst thing anyone could ever do is work at a job or in a career that they do not enjoy for a long period of time. Money can buy many things. However, money cannot buy the time back that is wasted working. Money cannot buy the time back that you spent clocking in at a job that has no growth. Money cannot buy back the time you wasted earning a degree just to get a job to make enough to pay back those student loans.

So like I told my niece: It's your life, go live it doing what you want.

If you want to build items out of pallets and call it a business, then go at it 100%. If you want to start an organic garden planting business, then do so, and do it no matter what anyone has to say. If you want to own a photography business, then learn all you can about photography and be the best. Like I said before, there is someone making fortune taking photos. And if you want to take photos for a living then why can't that person be you? Because every passion can converted to a business you can make your passion your business, which means you will make a living doing what you love.

Now if you know what you want to do, but do not know where to get started, please allow me to help you. Discover how my book will help get the results you desire, and make the rest of your life the best of your life.

I am Shawn Ousley, Follow Your Passion / Follow Your Dream

How to be Happy & Successful at the Same Damn Time by **Shawn Ousley**

Do you have a passion for something? What if you could turn that passion into a business? Let me show you how you could be happy and successful at the same damn time. I would like you to get a pen and paper to write down a few things. If you don't have pen and paper with you, read the entire blog post first then come back.

At the top of the paper write your passion. Makeup. Baking. Lawn Care. Child Care. Writing. Blogging. Car Care. Whatever your passion write it down at the top of the page. Now on the next line write one of the following Goal Statements or one similar that works for you:

Goal Statement 1:
How I can make $_____ by _____ (date) by doing _____.

Goal Statement 2:
Steps needed to achieve _____ by _____ (date), and earning $_____ a year.

Goal Statement 3:
Ways to get into the top 10% of my field by _____ (date).

Now to the easy, yet hard part.

Number each line 1 through 20. Next, write something on each line that will get you to your goal. You may write something like get a web site, buy business cards, go talk to a certain type of business, visit realtors, make referrals, etc.. Make sure you write a step or action to be taken on each of the lines.

I call this the LIST 20. Why? For the reason that you are going to list twenty steps/actions that need to be taken to make you successful and happy.

The next step is the most important part of the List 20. That is to make sure you do something every day that is on your list. Every single day. Not some days. Not weekends. Not off days. Every day. Even if that something is reading 30 minutes about your subject, then do that. (The matter of reading in your field is a whole other beast in and of itself.) Remember, the objective is to achieve your Goal Statement.

It has been proven that individuals who do what they love for a living never feel like they ever work. Ask a radio DJ who loves working in radio if he ever feels like he is actually working. Ask an artist who makes a living drawing and painting if they ever feel like they are working. There's an old saying that says "Find what you love to do and then find someone to pay you to do it." That statement sums up the title of this blog post: How to be happy and successful at the same damn time.

My son loves cars. He watches shows where business owners buy old cars. Then they fix, fabricate, and rebuild the cars to sell for profit. He loves to watch the car auctions. He will read any auto magazine that he can get his hands on. I asked him what he wanted to do when he grew up and he stated that he wanted to own his own mechanic shop. I have asked him this for 2 years now, and he gives the same answer each time. I know that he will be happy and successful owning a mechanic shop so because that is what he wants to do. More importantly, that is what he loves to do. He already has his List 20 started and he is only 12 years old.

I write about setting goals and many other subjects in my book Opportunistic Millionaire: Bringing Out Your Passion to Succeed.

I am Shawn Ousley, Follow Your Passion / Follow Your Dream

GOAL STATEMENTS

A Goal Statement has 3 parts
1 - A stated goal, which can be a dollar
amount of an achievement.
2 - An action word to achieve goal.
3 - A stated completion date.

Goal Statement #1

How I can make $_____ by
_____ (date) by doing _____.

Goal Statement #2

Steps needed to achieve _____
by _____ (date), and earning
$_____ a year.

Goal Statement #3

Ways to get into the top
10% of my field by __ (date)

IAMSHAWNOUSLEY.COM

i am Shawn Ousley
PO Box 88
Ida, LA 71044

Contact Information

Readers are encouraged to contact me with comments and questions. Use the same methods to contact me for bookings and speaking engagements.

Website   iamShawnOusley.com

E-mail   Shawn@iamShawnOusley.com

Facebook   facebook.com/iamShawnOusley

Twitter   @iamShawnOusley

Mail   Shawn Ousley
               PO Box 88
               Ida, LA 71044

www.ingramcontent.com/pod-product-compliance
Lightning Source LLC
Chambersburg PA
CBHW021437170526
45164CB00001B/287